YOU

WRITTEN BY KOBI YAMADA · DESIGNED BY SARAH FORSTER

You are
ONE OF A KIND.

UNIQUE YOU.

YOU MATTER

more than you know.

SIGNIFICANT YOU.

You are such

A GOOD PERSON.

ADMIRABLE YOU.

YOU
ARE SO
BIG-HEARTED.

GENEROUS YOU.

THERE IS CARING

in everything you do.

COMPASSIONATE YOU.

You have a wonderful way
WITH OTHERS.

CONSIDERATE YOU.

YOU SHARE
your gifts generously.

GIVING YOU.

You live each day

WITH INTENTION.

PURPOSEFUL YOU.

THE WORLD IS A BETTER PLACE BECAUSE YOU ARE IN IT.

REMARKABLE YOU.

YOU SEEK OUT WAYS

to give back and to help out.

THOUGHTFUL YOU.

You look for
THE GOOD IN LIFE.

POSITIVE YOU.

YOU BRING

a fresh perspective to any situation.

ORIGINAL YOU.

You

MAKE A DIFFERENCE.

HELPFUL YOU.

LIKING
YOU
IS EASY TO DO.

WONDERFUL YOU.

YOU EMBRACE LIFE

wholeheartedly.

ENTHUSIASTIC YOU.

You spread
HAPPINESS.

JOYFUL YOU.

YOU ADD LIGHT
wherever you go.

BRILLIANT YOU.

You are such
A POSITIVE INFLUENCE.

INSPIRING YOU.

THE WORLD NEEDS MORE PEOPLE LIKE YOU.

GENUINE YOU.

YOU ARE GIFTED

in so many ways.

TALENTED YOU.

You welcome new challenges
AND OPPORTUNITIES.

ADVENTUROUS YOU.

YOU ARE
willing to take chances.

COURAGEOUS YOU.

There is just so much to
APPRECIATE ABOUT YOU.

INCREDIBLE YOU.

YOU
MAKE THINGS
LOOK EASY.

CAPABLE YOU.

YOU FIND
possibilities everywhere.

RESOURCEFUL YOU.

You are really good
AT WHAT YOU DO.

AMAZING YOU.

THERE

is no one like you.

EXTRAORDINARY YOU.

COMPENDIUM.

live inspired

WITH SPECIAL THANKS TO THE ENTIRE COMPENDIUM FAMILY.

CREDITS:

Written by: KOBI YAMADA

Designed by: SARAH FORSTER

Edited by: NICOLE BURNS ASCUE AND AMELIA RIEDLER

Creative Direction by: JULIE FLAHIFF

ISBN: 978-1-938298-75-2

1st printing. Printed in China with soy inks.